Contents

What Are Micro Bugs?

We see animals and insects every day. But did you know there are millions of bugs that you can only see under a microscope? Right this minute they're probably crawling on you!

Micro bugs were first seen in the 1670s by Dutchman Antony van Leeuwenhoek.

MITES

The biggest family of microscopic animals are the mites. Most mites are less than 1 mm in length!

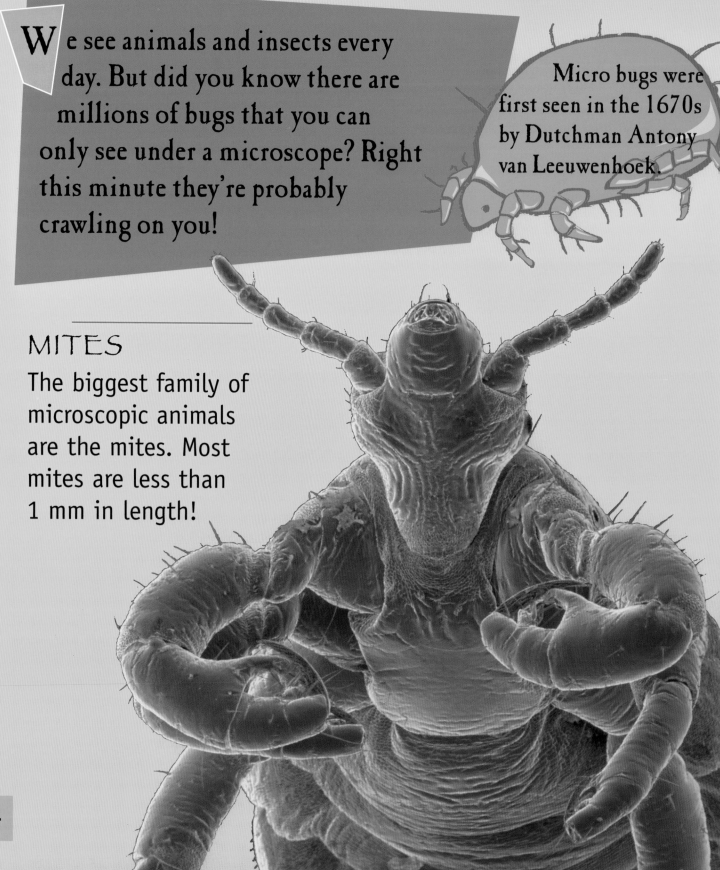

UP CLOSE

MICRO BUGS

PAUL HARRISON

W
FRANKLIN WATTS
LONDON•SYDNEY

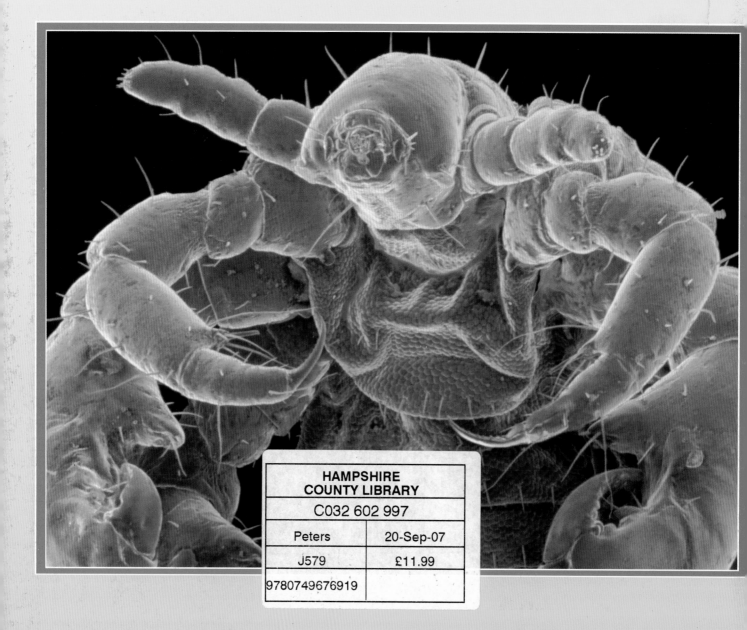

Published in 2007 by Franklin Watts

Copyright © 2007 Arcturus Publishing Limited

Franklin Watts
338 Euston Road
London NW1 3BH

Franklin Watts Australia
Level 17/207 Kent Street
Sydney, NSW 2000

Author: Paul Harrison
Editor (new edition): Ella Fern
Designers (new edition): Steve West, Steve Flight

Picture credits: NHPA: 8 bottom; Science Photo Library: front and back cover, title page, 2, 4, 5 top, middle, bottom, 6, 7 top, bottom, 8 top, 9, 10 top, bottom, 11, 12, 13 top, bottom, 14, 15 top, bottom, 16, 17, 18, 19 top, middle, 20, 21 top, middle.

A CIP catalogue record for this book is available from the British Library

Dewey number: 579

ISBN: 978-0-7496-7691-9

Printed in China

Franklin Watts is a division of Hachette Children's Books.

BUGS

Of course, not all the microscopic marvels that you'll find in this book are mites. There are lots of other bugs that you can only see under a microscope.

MICROSCOPE

The study of micro bugs really took off when the electron microscope was invented in 1931. Ernst Ruska, who invented it, was awarded the Nobel Prize in 1986.

NEMATODES

Nematodes are like extremely small worms. Scientists aren't sure how many species of nematodes there are. They believe only a small number of the different varieties have been discovered so far.

Tiny Tenants

I n the past, houses used to be riddled with micro bugs. Today, our houses are much cleaner, but there will still be mites lurking somewhere...

BED AND BREAKFAST

Are you aware that you might be sharing your bed at night? Bed bugs love to hide in mattresses and feed on people's blood when they're asleep.

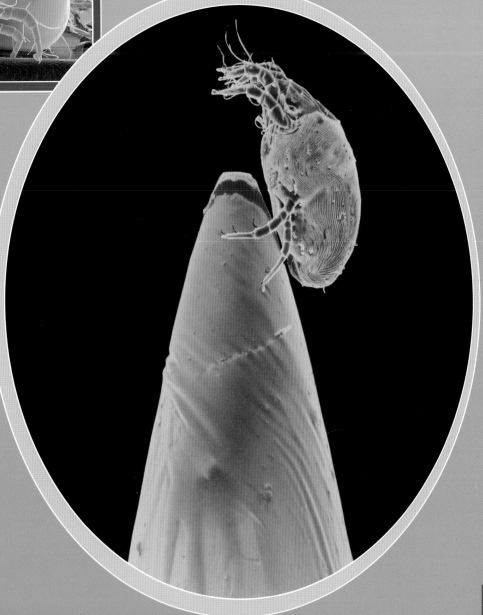

FLAKY

Thankfully, most beds don't have bed bugs, but they do have dust mites. These mites live all around the house, though most of them are found in beds. This is because beds are full of tiny bits of people's skin flakes—and this is what mites eat.

MITEY CLIMB

This dust mite has made it up to the top of a needle.
The picture gives you an idea of how big—or how small—it is.

7

FOOD FOR FRIENDS

Food mites are often very pale in colour. They measure less than 0.5 mm long and can be found on cheese, flour, sugar and cereals. Yum!

BOOKISH

Although they are called book lice, these leggy lice will eat a whole range of foods, not just books. They love warm and humid environments, especially libraries.

Keep an eye on your books—especially this one!

Personal Parasites

W ith so many tiny bugs and mites out there it's not really surprising that your body is home to whole of host of micro monsters too.

HAIR RAISING

Head lice, or nits, camp out in your hair. They're only around 2 mm long, but that doesn't mean they aren't annoying.

LOUSY BODY

The body louse lives on peoples' bodies and clothes. It doesn't like cleanliness much, so having a bath's a good idea.

EYE EYE

Believe it or not, there's even a type of mite that lives on your eyelashes! It's called the follicle mite.

CLOSE-UP

Follicle mites are less than 0.5 mm long!

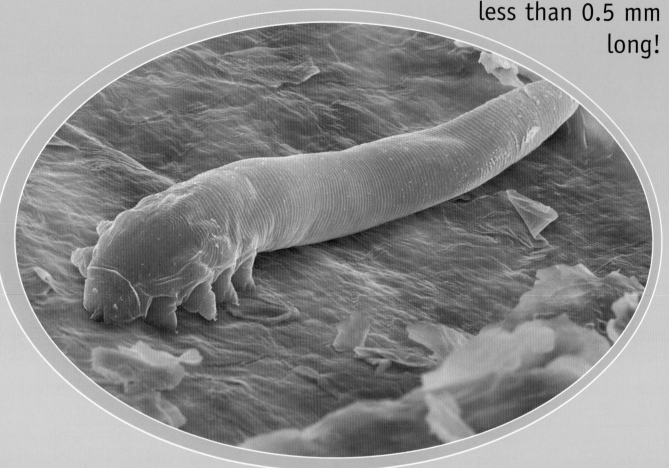

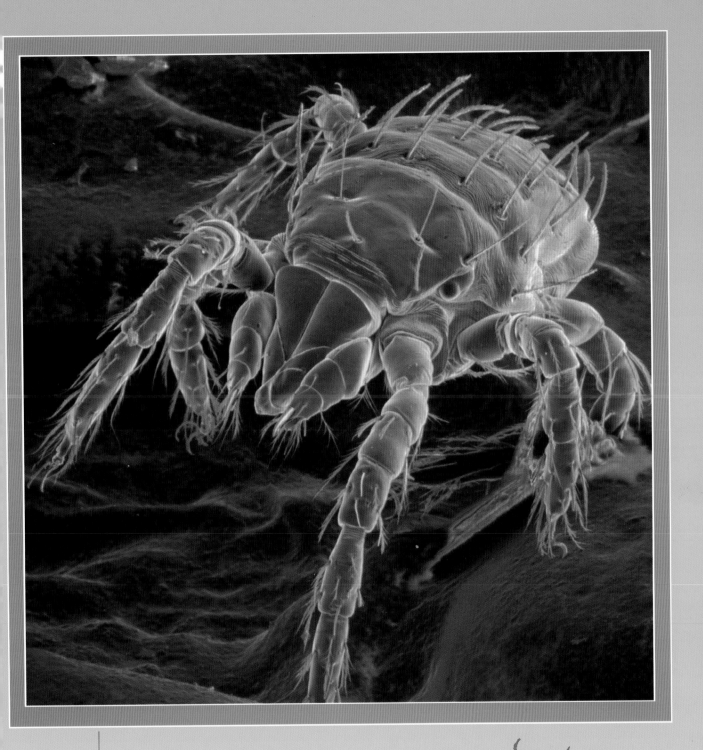

ITCHY

Little mites can sometimes cause big problems. This one is a baby red mite. They sometimes bite adults, leaving itchy sores.

The horrible scabies mite can actually burrow into your skin!

11

Animal Antics

A nimals are attacked by far more tiny terrors than we humans, and the results can be fatal for them.

JUMP TO IT

One parasite you may have encountered before is the flea. Fleas often live on cats and dogs. Under an electron microscope you can really see what these jumpy little blighters look like.

One type of mite likes to live on cats' ears!

12

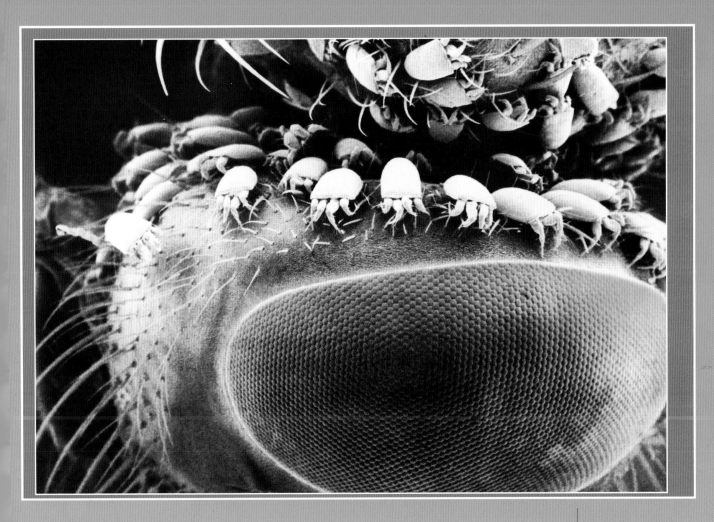

FOWL MITE
Fowl mites live on chickens and suck their blood, causing irritation. They can even reduce the number of eggs a chicken can lay.

BEE MITE
Even bees have tiny insects using them as a free lunch! Varroa mites and the tracheal mites can kill bees by sucking their blood.

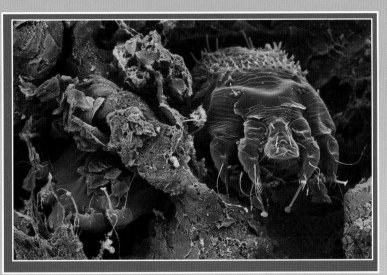

MANGY MUTT
Animals with mange (infected by mites) suffer from itchiness, hair loss and weight loss.

Plant Pests

If you thought the garden might be a place of refuge from micro bugs, think again—it's packed with them!

WORMY FEEDERS

Shoot nematodes live inside leaves and can cause them to lose colour or die. Other nematodes attack the roots of plants, slowing down growth.

GALLING

Have you ever
seen a plant with
odd looking lumps
and bumps that
don't seem to
belong to it?
They're called galls
and they're caused
by—you guessed
it—micro bugs!

FOOD FOR LIFE

Some galls, such as bud
galls and velvet galls, are
formed by mites feeding.
Up to eight generations of
mites are born each year.
Most spend their whole
lives inside the gall.

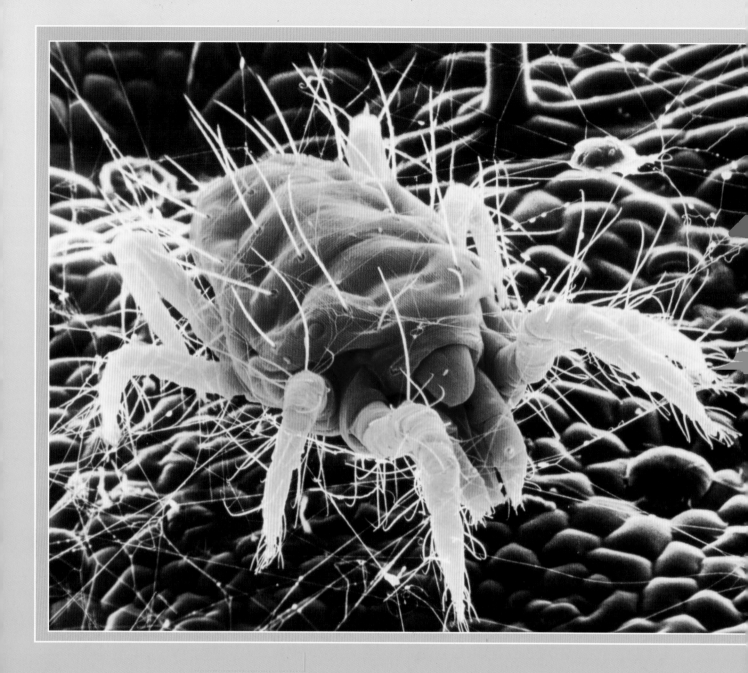

GOURMET

Gardeners hate red spider mites because they like to eat all the things you do, like strawberries and peas.

Red spider mites only turn red during the autumn and winter.

SPRING BREAK

Some mites, such as the clover mite, like nothing better than the taste of fresh young seedlings. They can be found in large numbers in early spring.

Tiniest of All

The smallest micro bugs of all are called microbes. Microbes can be found everywhere. There are so many of them in the world your head would explode just thinking about it.

MOVERS AND SHAKERS

Protozoa are the microbes on the move. Some get about by beating a long thin tail, like a tadpole.

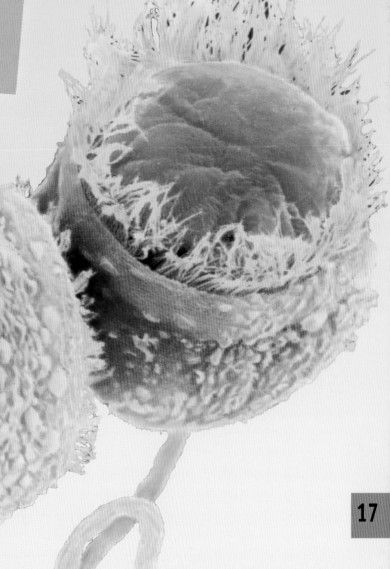

JUST ROTTEN

The fungus family doesn't just include mushrooms. Two of the smallest members of the family are moulds and yeast, which you need to bake bread.

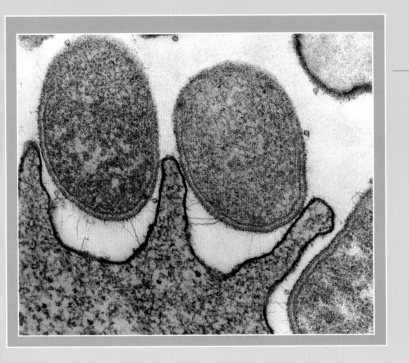

BACTERIA

Of all the microbes the most numerous are bacteria. They can be found in water, in the soil and on animals and people. Bacteria come in all sorts of shapes and sizes.

DEAD OR ALIVE

One controversial member of the microbe clan is the virus. There is some debate as to whether viruses are living things or not. But one thing viruses can definitely do is make you feel unwell.

Scientists have found fossils of microbes dating back around 3.5 million years.

Good Bug, Bad Bug

M icro bugs can be bad for your health. But sometimes these tiny critters can be very useful indeed.

One type of microbe lives inside termites' stomachs, helping them to digest wood.

NOT-SO-SUPER

One of the scariest types of microbes are the super bugs. These are bacteria which are able to resist doctors' attempts to kill them off with antibiotics. The most famous super bugs are MRSA and E-coli.

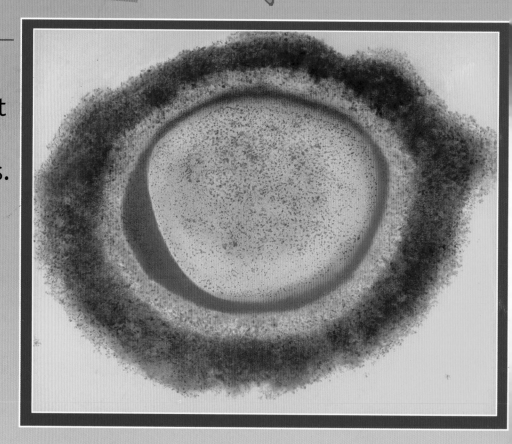

GARDEN FRIEND OR FOE

Nematodes can be bad news for plants. But some are so useful at eating other problem insects that gardeners actually buy them.

CLEANING UP

There are some types of bacteria which will eat petrol and oil. These bacteria can be used to help reduce the impact of oil spills.

GUT FEELING

One of the really useful things microbes do is help us to digest our food. Each person has over 10 trillion microbes in their body.

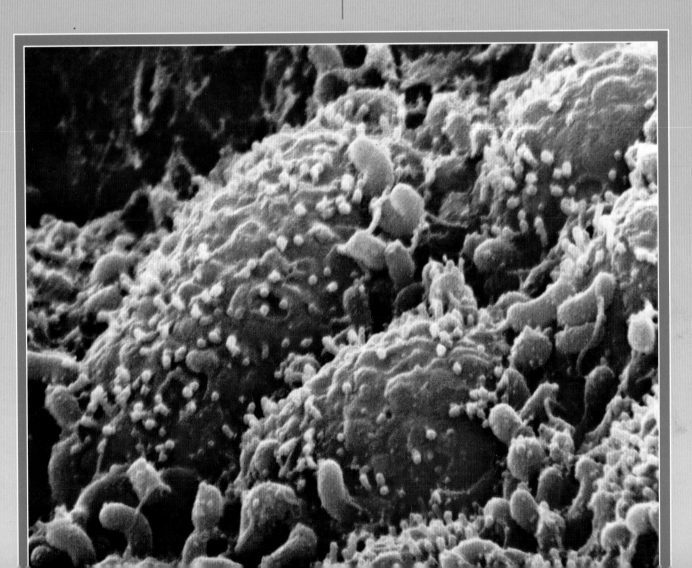

Glossary

Bacteria
Microscopic cells that can cause disease, but also help with processes like digestion and decomposition.

Ernst Ruska (1906-1988)
The scientist who invented the electron microscope in 1933.

Flea
A minute blood-sucking parasite that lives on the skin of animals and birds.

Follicles
Small cavities on the body that contain or protect each hair.

Gall
Abnormal growth on a tree or plant caused by bacteria or fungi.

Infested
When a human or animal is covered in mites or lice.

Louse (plural: lice)
A tiny blood-sucking parasite.

Mange
A skin infection caused by mites that causes hair loss. Mange mostly affects domestic animals.

Microbe
A microscopic organism.

Microscopic
Something that is not visible to the naked eye, and must be looked at using a microscope.

Mite
A tiny blood-sucking parasite.

Nematode
A tiny worm-like bug that lives outside.

Nit
A head louse that lays eggs in people's hair.

Parasite
A bug (or other animal or plant) that lives on another animal or plant and feeds off it.

Protozoa
A type of microbe.

Super bug
A bug like E-coli or MRSA that cannot be killed by antibiotics.

Virus
A microbe not even visible under a microscope that can cause disease.

Further Reading

The Best Book of Bugs
Claire Llewellyn, Kingfisher, 2005

The Big Book of Bugs
Theresa Greenaway, Dorling Kindersley,
2002

Bugs and Minibeasts
John Farndon, Southwater Books, 2002

Bug Hunters
Barbara Taylor, Chrysalis Children's
Books, 2003

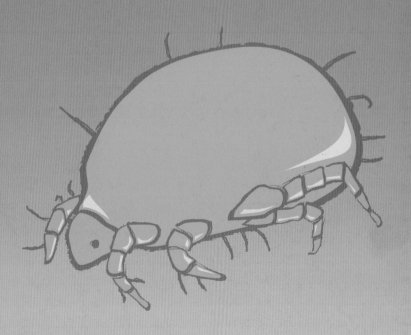

Index